Under The Radar
The College Scholarship Handbook
By Stephen Twizere

Contents

Preface:

Preface

A college scholarship -- every kid who plays sports dreams of one. Whether it is for recognition of sporting excellence, a cheaper way to get a university education or having your eyes fixed on the big leagues, one thing is for sure. They are extremely difficult to come by. I am fortunate enough to be in a position where I can help aspiring youngsters take the necessary steps to get just that little bit closer to achieving a collegiate scholarship. The focus of this book will be placed on college basketball in the US with some mention of college hoops in Canada. Now this book will not guarantee any success, but it will help you understand how scholarships work and what you can do to put yourself in position to be one of the lucky few.

The biggest reason I wanted to write this book is because I was once one of those kids who had dreams of getting a college scholarship. I'm not ashamed to admit that I had dreams of going one better and actually making the NBA. I was just an innocent kid from London, England with a dream. I felt that if I worked hard enough, and did my best, that would surely be enough to make my dreams come true. How wrong I was, though. I didn't have a clue. How many times have you heard someone tell you, "Be realistic, that's never going to happen"? If you have that mentality, you will not achieve even a fraction of what you're capable of. I have always believed it takes great courage to have a dream, people will always doubt you and try to put a limit on your ambitions. Having a dream is the first step to achieving the unknown, the will to strive for more is something I will always support. There is one condition, however, you need a blueprint for: how you plan to go about your dreams.

So often, we are told that if you are good enough, schools and coaches will find you. What does being good enough actually mean? Why wait for schools to discover you? Is there anything you can do to get noticed? The answer to that is yes. You may be one of those individuals who are trying to figure out everything all by yourself. You may be headed in the right direction, or maybe you don't even know where to begin. I want you to understand something. Whether you're hoping to get a scholarship or be the best player you can be, it requires a lot of planning and preparation. It certainly does not happen overnight. It takes a huge amount of commitment and determination.

It was not until after I was done playing that I was able to see what mistakes were made and what I could have done differently to give myself a better shot. One thing I learned is that mistakes need to happen in order to progress. Throughout this book, you will have a better understanding of everything that goes into getting a scholarship. You will be looking at it through the lens of an ambitious, yet naïve, kid out of the United Kingdom, looking to make his hoop dreams a reality.

My story was an interesting one and, might I add, a very insightful one. It seemed the closer I got to my goals, the harder the obstacles appeared. Before I called it a day on my playing dreams, I nearly quit many times before that. The passion I had for the game just wouldn't let me walk away that soon, but there came a time when I had a realisation of what was ahead for me. Sometimes the hardest thing to do is to be honest with yourself; but, at the same time, it is the best thing you can do for yourself. As you embark on your journey, there will be many pivotal tests and trials that will make you question why you are even pursuing your goals in the first place. The setbacks will reveal a lot about yourself, and there will be many times when you will be at a crossroads in your dreams. Will you quit or will you overcome the barrier that is in front of you? One day, I had a different response to this ultimatum.

I have no regret about my journey playing the game of basketball and why I cut the dream so abruptly. All basketball players know the amount of dedication and sacrifice that goes into chasing your dreams. So, for me to say that the decision to stop playing was an easy one, would be a flat out lie. I do, however, stand by my statement that I have no regrets. I was blessed with the opportunity to travel to the US for 2 years and play basketball. One year playing Prep Basketball in Texas, and my freshman year at a college in California. It was the first day of freshman year that I realised, I had got it all wrong. I was not at the level required to have success at the collegiate level and I am at peace with that. Do I feel that had I prepared differently prior to that season things would be different? It's very possible. I felt that I was going through this whole journey alone at times, no guidance and no point of reference. Just a young kid, trying to do what he can to be the next big thing.

Don't worry. This book isn't an autobiography on my life highlighting my successes and shortcomings. Through my story and journey, I hope that you can not only have the confidence to chase your dreams but be in a great position to make them happen. One of the things this book will discuss is having the right people around you to guide you through the process. This is something I did not have, but with this book, no need to worry. We've got you covered.

Chapter 1: Hoop Dreams

Remember the first time picking up that basketball. For many, it was love at first sight. Going to your local outdoor court and envisioning yourself draining the game winning shot before the buzzer sounds, the crowd screaming, players hugging you. Good times. Remember it like it was yesterday. You might still recreate that scene to this day. Well, believe it or not, that little moment right there is extremely powerful. We've all heard the saying, "you have to see it to believe it." It's kind of true. Before achieving anything, you have to imagine it happening first and believe that it can be done. That's probably real motivational for you to hear right now. Believe me, I've heard it plenty of times. Something that's equally important is knowing and being aware of what opportunities are out there for you. What can you do to put yourself in the best position to land a scholarship? How do you get noticed and recognised to the point where you are a scholarship-type player? Before all of that, I want to ask you a question: how many levels for college basketball are you aware of? Take your time now. List as many as you can.

Okay, so you were probably able to name the more well-known levels -- NCAA Division I, II, III, NJCAA Division I, II, III and NAIA Division I & II. If you were able to name these, then you're on the right track. It is really important that you're familiar with what is available to you. Not only what's available, but also the differences between the varying levels and the specific expectations of each one. There are actually a total of 16 different levels for college basketball -- 14 in the US & 2 in Canada. Surprised? Not to worry. The levels mentioned above are the most common. Below is the full list, in no particular order:

USA

NCAA
Division I, II, III

NJCAA
Division I, II, III

NAIA
Division I, II

National Christian College Athletic Association (NCCAA)
Division I, II

California Community College Athletic Association (CCCAA)

United States Collegiate Athletic Association (USCAA)

Northwest Athletic Conference (NWAC)

Association of Christian College Athletics (ACCA)
Canada

CCAA

U Sports

Surprise! There are more schools than just Duke, Kentucky and North Carolina. If I had a dollar for every time someone told me they wanted to go Division 1, I would be retired by now. Nothing wrong with being ambitious, but let's actually break down some numbers and figures, shall we?

Let's focus on NCAA Division I (DI) for a moment -- the epitome of college sports. The biggest crowds, the biggest following and an opportunity to play on national television. So, many reasons why players dream of reaching this level. Alright, so there are 353 Division I schools. That was not a typo. There really are that many. Each school has 13 scholarships to offer each year in Men's Basketball and 15 in Women's.

You're probably liking these odds at the moment. Let's look at how many high school basketball players are in the US alone. We're going to take figures from the 2018/2019 season.

For males, there were an astonishing 540,769 participants and for females 399,067. Out of the males, 18,816 participated in the NCAA. Out of the females, this figure was 16,509. Overall, this gave male high school players 3.5% chance to participate in the NCAA and female high school players a 4.1% chance.

Let's dive into this a little deeper and look at NCAA Division I & II specifically. From these figures, male high school players had a 1.0% chance of playing both Division I and Division II basketball. For female high school players, the chances of playing Division I had a 1.3% probability and a 1.2% probability for Division II. Are you surprised by these figures? Are they higher or lower than what you imagined? We focused on these 2 levels of NCAA as they offer athletic scholarships as well as academic, whilst NCAA Division III only offers academic-based scholarships.

Just a reminder this was in the US alone.

Can you imagine how large that number would be if we took figures from every country that plays basketball? Bear in mind, basketball is one of the fastest growing sports in the world today. Long story short, college basketball is no joke. You really have to be elite. There is no way around it. So, what can you do to even stand a chance of getting a look at playing college basketball? We will get into that shortly.

These figures are not intended to scare you or kill your dream. Just to give you the big picture of what the next level is all about. The good news is, many players receive opportunities to play college basketball every single year. The percentage of those receiving scholarships leads us to our next question: what is an Athletic College Scholarship?

This is one of the biggest misconceptions for high school players. People assume that every scholarship means that your tuition, room and board is 100% covered. Not quite. Well, in most cases, at least, this is not true. If you're a big time player, you can expect to receive a number of what we call "full ride" scholarship offers. This means that both your tuition and accommodations are covered. What you need to understand is, the amount of scholarships available all depends on the school's budget. Some schools generate a lot of money through their basketball program, so the amount of full-ride scholarships they can give is larger than other schools. One thing to also note is that a full ride does not necessarily mean you pay nothing. Quite often, you will still have to pay for your study books for your classes. These can often be more than $1,000 for the year. Sounds crazy, I know; but, believe me, those books do not come cheap. Might seem like a lot, but in comparison to the cost of tuition for the school, you better be grateful that you're not paying tuition. Oh, and did I mention that standard tuition is almost double for International students? Even more of an incentive to get that scholarship!

It is worth mentioning that not every level offers scholarships for sports. For example, the CCCAA in California does not offer scholarships. These schools are community colleges, also known as junior colleges, which allow you to attend for 2 years. There are other ways to get a reduction on tuition via financial aid, but this can be tricky for International Students. On the positive side, these schools are a lot cheaper in comparison to other levels. This is not a general rule for junior colleges. There are many that offer scholarships, but just not for schools in the CCCAA. Also, don't assume that a scholarship is for the duration of your academic career. Scholarships can be taken away after a season if you don't handle your business on the court as well as off it.

What to Expect at Each Level

So, you are up to speed with what options are available to you if you're hoping to play college hoops. But what are the expectations and the reality you can expect? We are going to focus primarily on 5 levels, NCAA (Div. I & II), NJCAA (Div. I) & NAIA (Div. I & II). These are the levels where schools are most likely to give out scholarships.

I'm going to give a quick ranking system between these schools in terms of level of play, with the first being the most competitive. These rankings are purely from a playing perspective:

1. NCAA Div. I
2. NJCAA Div. I
3. NCAA Div. II
4. NAIA Div. I
5. NAIA Div. II

NCAA Div. I

Some would argue that II & III are equal or interchangeable, but this is the list I've gone for, and I will explain why.

Let's start with NCAA Div. I.

As we saw, the chances of playing Div.I basketball are very slim, let alone receiving a scholarship. Div. I hoops are considered the toughest level to play. This is where the majority of the top players in the world play their college basketball. This is not to say that the other levels are not tough, but they don't quite compare to Div. I. There are many reasons kids target Division I basketball, one of them being that it would give them the best shot of continuing their basketball career after college. Whether that be the NBA, Europe or even South America, many see Division I as an avenue to get to the Pros. Division I hoops, as a whole, has the best college players in the country, and it generates the most money, by far, in comparison to other levels. With TV deals, jersey sales and even fans, it really is at the top of college sports. They have also introduced a system where elite high school seniors can earn money off their likeness and popularity once they enter the NCAA. This goes for well-known players with a large social media following. We can talk all day about the so-called "clout" that comes with Division I, but let's look at the playing side of things.

The NBA drafts a large percentage of their players from NCAA Division I, so you already know that the competition is going to be fierce. Division I basketball is the home of players with many accolades, from High School Gatorade Player of the Year winners to players who have had success at an International level. This does not mean you can't play at this level if you're not one of these kids, but it's worth noting, as every other game you are likely to face one of these players, depending on which conference your school plays in. We're going to get into the specific requirements of your game in the next chapter, but just know that the standard in Division I is extremely high.

NJCAA DIV I
NJCAA Division I is the highest level of junior college or "Juco" as most refer to it as. Now, remember, junior colleges are only 2-year schools. So, from an academic standpoint, they don't fare with the other levels; but, from a playing standpoint, it's up there with the best of them.

You may have heard some people refer to Juco as a "dog fight." In some ways, this is true. Players who attend Junior College only see it as a platform to move up, they have their sights on progressing after 1 or 2 years. With this mentality, it provides some of the most competitive environments around. For many players, it's all or nothing; so, they play with an extra chip on their shoulder. Junior College hosts players from all kinds of backgrounds. Some who had fallen off track during their high school career, and others who maybe didn't meet the grade or test requirements for the NCAA. That said, Juco produces a lot NCAA Division I talent, especially in the NJCAA Div. I. You may find players who are extremely athletic but not quite polished, or players who are highly skilled but lack the physical tools to compete in the NCAA Division I.

Many view Junior College as an opportunity to develop and improve in weaker areas. Coaches in the NCAA recruit transfers from Junior Colleges every year. There have been a number of NBA players who started off at Junior Colleges and ended up picking scholarships to Division I schools, so you know the level is respected. The fact that many see Junior College as a second chance or a ticket to the next level is why I put it slightly ahead of NCAA Division II in terms of talent.

NCAA Division II
NCAA Division II is a very respectable level and is, by no means, easy. The drop off, in terms of talent, is not huge from DI to DII. You find a lot of high level players in this division. It arguably has a more structured style of play than the Junior College levels. The academic requirements

are higher for DII schools in comparison to Jucos. Some DII schools face Division I schools in the pre-season, and are competitive in these games.

So, what is the main difference with DI & DII, Division I players? The players are typically bigger and more athletic than Division II prospects. Division II schools do not get the allure or hype Division I schools receive. Many Division II standouts receive opportunities to play professionally every year, so you can be confident that the level is regarded highly -- not just in the US, but also on a global scale. If you were one of those people who felt that it would be easy to gain a Division II scholarship, you are truly mistaken.

NAIA Division I
This is where we see a slight dip in level. NAIA may still be a fast-paced environment, in comparison to basketball in Europe, but you won't have as many big names playing at this level. The top teams in NAIA could compete with more of the low major NCAA DII schools, but that's likely as far as it would go.

NAIA Division II is not too different from NAIA Division I; but, NAIA DI has slightly more competition. Both levels offer scholarships, but how much money the school offers depends greatly on your academic capabilities for NAIA. Coaches expect their players to be capable. There are some instances where players from Division II drop to play NAIA basketball. We often see many standout Junior College players attending NAIA schools after 2 years. NAIA offers players a chance to get a solid education whilst competing at a respectable level. At this level, you see less making it as professionals than the other levels, but it is not impossible. Especially if you're able to produce at a high rate. I've come across many professional players who played NAIA for 4 years, and they are some of the better players I've met.

If you receive interest from one of these schools, never consider it as a weak level of competition.

NAIA Division II
NAIA Division II is a similar environment to NAIA DI, but the level of competition and athletes is slightly diminished. You will find the average height of positions slightly shorter and players slightly less athletic. Nevertheless, coaches still recruit and play to win, so not just anyone can attend these programs. The main difference between this level and the other levels mentioned is the end goal. A smaller majority of the players in this division have an aspiration to continue playing basketball after their studies. The experience of playing college sports is something that should never be taken for granted. So, this could be a good option for many of you.

What really matters
So, that summarises the most competitive levels in the US. Remember that aiming to reach the highest level is something I encourage, but don't aim to play somewhere you may not get opportunities. The most important thing is to have the opportunity to see the floor and contribute to the program. We're now going to take a look at basketball in Canada. Many are unaware of basketball in this part of the globe, myself included. So let's dive in!

Basketball in Canada

College basketball in Canada is not something I was aware of when growing up; but, had I known more about it, I would have considered it. The style of basketball in Canada is almost identical to that in the US. Fast-paced, up tempo and a lot of emphasis on defensive pressure. You can expect a whole lot if you are hoping to take your career out here. Canada, as a nation, has also risen to be one of the powerhouses in International basketball, recently challenging the US for the throne.

From a cultural standpoint, Canada has many similarities to Europe in terms of lifestyle, food and leisure. Canada is essentially the best of both worlds when comparing the US & Europe. There are a total of 129 men's programs and 125 women's programs, and the majority of them play in the CCAA or the U Sports Association. Simon Fraser University is the only Canadian program that competes outside of Canada. They are part of the NCAA (Division II).

Canada is definitely a location worth considering. There are some teams that can compete with NCAA Division I low major schools and the majority of Division II programs. In regards to the academic requirements, like most institutions, you need to maintain a respectable GPA – typically, a minimum of a 3.0. Most schools do not require you to have taken your SAT or ACT, but it's advisable to do so to ensure your options are not limited. Schools in Canada also offer scholarships, which is another great option and reason for you to consider Canada.

I hope that has made the levels of college basketball easier to understand. The next chapter will go into detail as to what is expected of you at the higher collegiate levels. For instance: what can you do on the court to prepare you to have as many opportunities available as possible.

Chapter 2
On the court: What is your why?

Why do you play the game of basketball? Are you passionate about the game, or wanting to make something out of it? There is a difference between doing something and having a reason for doing it. The reason you do something will definitely play a role in what you eventually end up achieving. With all things in life, it is important to have a purpose for what you do. Some refer to this as your "why." If you're trying to gain a scholarship to the US for basketball, you're a dedicated individual who spends countless hours trying to improve their craft. If that doesn't sound like you, then you're already behind. The minimum -- and I mean *minimum* -- you need to have is a great work ethic. Talent will only get you so far. The further you wanna go, the harder you will need to work. This doesn't only apply to sports. It's a rule of life.

Okay, so we can agree that hard work is a major contributor to any success; but, what actually is hard work? Many coaches have different ways to measure how hard someone works. Some base it on being punctual and doing everything they say. Others base it on how much effort you put in on any given day.

Imagine this scenario. Basketball pre-season has started. You're ready to show your worth and leave a good impression on the head coach. You're early to every session, give 110% in every drill and don't take any shortcuts during the workouts. After each day, you go home and rest.

Now a second scenario. Your team mate starts his day 2 hours before pre-season starts. When he wakes up, he does a 5K run before he's even had breakfast. He then heads to pre-season, training early and gets up 200 shots before practice has begun. During the pre-season training, he's still going harder than everyone else and giving 110% in each drill. When he goes home, he doesn't go to bed until he has completed 100 pushups, 100 sit ups and 100 squats.

Which person sounds like a hard worker? The second, of course. You were thinking the person in the first scenario, weren't you?. This is what I want you to understand. Hard work is relative. The first thing I ask any of my players before they train with me is, "Are you a hard worker?" All of them say yes. But, once the workout is finished, I can see many different results. This does not mean some of these players are not hard workers; they still took time out of their day to work on their game. It just shows that there are different levels to hard work.

If you want to be a hard worker, follow this principle: do more to improve your game than any other player on your team.

That is how you develop a "hardest worker in the room" mindset. At the same time, you can't only compare your efforts to the people in your circle. There are millions of people trying to get to the same destination as you. Coaches won't be impressed if you only turn up on time and try your best -- that is an expectation. It's the players who do more before practice, during practice and after practice who really separate themselves from the rest. That is how the mediocre become good, and the good become great.

Can you get some extra ball handling work in before the session starts? Can you do any additional cardio after practice ends? If so, do it. Don't waste time worrying or comparing yourselves to others. There is no time to get complacent.

One of the best ways to develop a "hard working mentality" is to get rid of your "being content mentality." So, let's say, you made 5 three pointers in practice today, and you're feeling good about yourself. Do you go to bed or are you going to spend an extra hour or two to work on your game even more? We all have choices to make, our progress depends on what we decide.

Quick story for you. One practice, during my prep year at a school in Houston, I was on fire. Like, I could not miss. I was hitting catch and shoot, step backs, and shooting off screens. You name it. Players were getting me hyped up and I'm not gonna lie -- I felt like the MAN after that practice. I went home and didn't do anything else for the rest of the day. The next day, my coach called me into his office and wanted to talk about the previous practice. I thought he was going to praise me for how well I did -- wrong. The first thing he asked me was if I did any extra work when I got home. Feeling ashamed, I responded, "No, sir." He questioned my desire and my mindset, then if I was content with how I performed in that practice session. He asked me if that's the highest level I wanted to reach and if I felt that great players take time off after they have one good game, let alone one good practice. This conversation spoke volumes to me and really opened my eyes to what is required of great players and success in the field.

How far you go is heavily dependent on how much extra work you're willing to put in. Are you only going to do extra work when you feel like it? When things aren't how you want them to be? With every single one of you, there is another level you can reach. Some of you have so much potential and don't even realise it. It's time for you to start exploring how great you can really be and it all begins with your mentality. The reason so many great players reach the heights they do, is simply because they have the mindset that they're the worst player on the team, and should, therefore, work the hardest. They're not satisfied with being the best player on their team, their school or their area. They have sights on being the best player of all time, but, without that mindset, you cannot become the best version of yourself. Your journey is pointless without hard work.

Let's get into the technicalities of what makes you a college-level player. The general basis of a college player is pretty similar across all boards in terms of what is expected by each position. The margin for error decreases the further you want to go. I am going to give you a rough position by position breakdown of some of the things a college player should be able to do.

Point Guard:

- Vocal leader
- High IQ
- Great facilitator
- Good ball handling skill set
- Can defend the perimeter
- Preferable if they can shoot the ball well from outside and inside

Shooting Guard:

- Shoots well from the outside (catch & shoot and off the dribble)
- Good ball handling skill set
- Can defend the perimeter
- Preferable if they are athletic
- Can finish well inside

Small Forward:

- Ability to knock down open shots from behind the arc
- Great in the open floor
- Can defend inside and outside
- Aggressive rebounder
- Preferable if they are athletic
- Can finish well inside

Power Forward:

- Ability to knock down a mid-range jump shot
- Preferable if they can shoot from behind the arc
- High IQ
- Can defend inside and possibly wings
- Ability to make a pass
- Aggressive rebounder
- Good finishing touch inside

Centres:

- Ability to knock down a mid-range jump shot
- Big plus if they can shoot from outside
- Ability to run the floor basket to basket
- Can defend inside
- Aggressive rebounder
- High IQ offensively and defensively
- Ability to finish inside

From this guideline, what do you notice? Every position has to be able to defend. So often, we fall in love with the offensive side of the game but pay little attention to the defensive side. If there is one thing I can't emphasise enough, it is the ability to stop your opposition. Forget about being able to shoot or score at college level. The first question you should ask is: can you *defend* at a college level? If you can't, then your chances of playing college basketball just decreased. I have good news, though. Being a good defender probably requires the least amount of skill in comparison to the offensive side of the game.

The Three Levels of Defence

What is defence exactly? Well, it has different levels – good, great and elite.

A good defender is able to contain and slow down an offensive player. I'm sure you've had games where you haven't been scored on that much and felt you have done a good job.

A great defender not only contains their opposition, but reduces their chances of being able to create for others. Great defenders are able to get deflections and steal the ball.

Elite defenders disrupt the whole flow of the offence. They not only make it hard for the offensive player to dribble the ball, but also mess up their whole rhythm. Limiting the player's touches, making it difficult for them to get a clear look at the basket, etc. Elite defenders are always a step ahead. Being a solid defender starts with a mindset and a desire to make sure the opposition works twice as hard against you than any other player. You may see many of your favourite defensive players getting hyped after making big time defensive plays. These players are locked in before the whistle even blows. The best defender will always have a place on the team, so make this an area of focus.

Mindset Exercise

This activity is going to require you to write something down. So make sure you have a pen and paper ready. I want you to now put yourself in the mindset of a coach and really analyse your game. Think about what you're good at, not so great at and where you hope your game can be in a year's time. You can list as many things as possible. Your list might include different skills based on the position you play, how tall you are or how long you have been playing. Not to worry, everyone starts somewhere, but it is helpful to know what you should be working towards.

Below is a table for you to keep track of different skills you should be able to or are expected to do before joining any college basketball team. The ones with a star symbol (★) are non-negotiable, the ones with a check symbol (✓) are preferable and the ones without anything are not necessarily required, but are a bonus if you are able to do them. Please note that this will vary for your position, height and age, but, by the time you are 18, these are what will be expected from a college coach when recruiting you.

Progress tracker for Point Guards (Men's Basketball)
Average Height NCAA DIV I: 6'1+
DIV II: 6'0+

Name:
Age:
Height:
Weight:
Position:

Skill	Week 1	Week 2	Week 3	Week 4	Week 5	Week 6	Week 7	Week 8
Layup with both ★								
Dribble with both★								
Passing with both★								
Catch & shoot mid-range★								
Off the dribble mid-range★								
Catch & Shoot 3 Pointer✓								
Off the dribble 3 Pointer✓								
Free Throws★								
1 hand dunk✓								
2 hand dunk								

Progress tracker for Shooting Guards (Men's Basketball)
Average Height NCAA DIV I: 6'3+
* DIV II: 6'2+*

Name:
Age:
Height:
Weight:
Position:

Skill	Week 1	Week 2	Week 3	Week 4	Week 5	Week 6	Week 7	Week 8
Layup with both★								
Dribble with both★								
Passing with both★								
Catch & shoot mid-range★								
Off the dribble mid-range★								
Catch & Shoot 3 Pointer★								
Off the dribble 3 Pointer★								
Free Throws★								
1 hand dunk ✓								
2 hand dunk✓								

Progress tracker for Small Forwards (Men's Basketball)
Average height NCAA DIV I: 6'5+
DIV II: 6'4+

Name:
Age:
Height:
Weight:
Position:

Skill	Week 1	Week 2	Week 3	Week 4	Week 5	Week 6	Week 7	Week 8
Layup with both★								
Dribble with both★								
Passing with both★								
Catch & shoot mid-range★								
Off the dribble midrange★								
Catch & Shoot 3 Pointer★								
Off the dribble 3 Pointer								
Free Throws✓								
1 hand dunk★								
2 hand dunk★								

Progress tracker for Power Forwards (Men's Basketball)
Average Height NCAA DIV I: 6'7+
NCAA DIV II: 6'6+

Name:

Age:

Height:

Weight:

Position:

Skill	Week 1	Week 2	Week 3	Week 4	Week 5	Week 6	Week 7	Week 8
Layup with both★								
Dribble with both★								
Passing with both★								
Catch & shoot mid-range★								
Off the dribble mid-range✓								
Catch & Shoot 3 Pointer✓								
Off the dribble 3 Pointer								
Free Throws★								
1 hand dunk★								
2 hand dunk★								

Progress tracker for Centres (Men's Basketball)
Average Height NCAA DIV I: 6'9+
NCAA DIV II: 6'8+

Name:
Age:
Height:
Weight:
Position:

Skill	Week 1	Week 2	Week 3	Week 4	Week 5	Week 6	Week 7	Week 8
Layup with both ★								
Dribble with both ✓								
Passing with both ✓								
Catch & shoot mid-range ★								
Off the dribble midrange								
Catch & Shoot 3 Pointer								
Off the dribble 3 Pointer								
Free Throws ★								
1 hand dunk ★								
2 hand dunk ★								

Progress tracker for Point Guards (Women's Basketball)
Average Height NCAA DIV I: 5'8+
NCAA DIV II: 5'6+

Name:
Age:
Height:
Weight:
Position:

Skill	Week 1	Week 2	Week 3	Week 4	Week 5	Week 6	Week 7	Week 8
Layup with both★								
Dribble with both★								
Passing with both★								
Catch & shoot mid-range★								
Off the dribble mid-range★								
Catch & Shoot 3 Pointer★								
Off the dribble 3 Pointer★								
Free Throws★								
1 hand dunk								
2 hand dunk								

Progress tracker for Shooting Guards (Women's Basketball)
Average Height NCAA DIV I: 5'10+
NCAA DIV II: 5'8+

Name:
Age:
Height:
Weight:
Position:

Skill	Week 1	Week 2	Week 3	Week 4	Week 5	Week 6	Week 7	Week 8
Layup with both★								
Dribble with both★								
Passing with both★								
Catch & shoot mid-range★								
Off the dribble mid-range★								
Catch & Shoot 3 Pointer★								
Off the dribble 3 Pointer★								
Free Throws★								
1 hand dunk								
2 hand dunk								

Progress tracker for Small Forwards (Women's Basketball)
Average Height NCAA DIV I: 5'11+
NCAA DIV II: 5'10+

Name:
Age:
Height:
Weight:
Position:

Skill	Week 1	Week 2	Week 3	Week 4	Week 5	Week 6	Week 7	Week 8
Layup with both★								
Dribble with both★								
Passing with both★								
Catch & shoot mid range★								
Off the dribble mid range★								
Catch & Shoot 3 Pointer★								
Off the dribble 3 Pointer✓								
Free Throws★								
1 hand dunk								
2 hand dunk								

Progress tracker for Power Forwards (Women's Basketball)
Average Height NCAA DIV I: 6'0+
NCAA DIV II: 5'11+

Name:

Age:

Height:

Weight:

Position:

Skill	Week 1	Week 2	Week 3	Week 4	Week 5	Week 6	Week 7	Week 8
Layup with both★								
Dribble with both★								
Passing with both★								
Catch & shoot mid range★								
Off the dribble mid range✔								
Catch & Shoot 3 Pointer✔								
Off the dribble 3 Pointer								
Free Throws★								
1 hand dunk								
2 hand dunk								

Progress tracker for Centres (Women's Basketball)
Average Height NCAA DIV I: 6'2+
NCAA DIV II:6'0+

Name:
Age:
Height:
Weight:
Position:

Skill	Week 1	Week 2	Week 3	Week 4	Week 5	Week 6	Week 7	Week 8
Layup with both★								
Dribble with both✔								
Passing with both✔								
Catch & shoot mid range★								
Off the dribble mid range								
Catch & Shoot 3 Pointer								
Off the dribble 3 Pointer								
Free Throws★								
1 hand dunk								
2 hand dunk								

These tables should help you have a better idea of what is required to be considered a college-ready prospect. Typically, as the standard drops, there is less of a requirement to be taller, but it does not mean that if you are slightly smaller than the average you won't be able to receive a scholarship. You may, however, have to work slightly harder than those taller than you.

One thing that doesn't get compromised is skill level. You have to be a high-level player to receive a scholarship for basketball at any level. Think about it, every college roster is made up of the best high school players on each team. This means that once you enter college, you're going up against players that have accolades, won titles, have broken school records and received recognition for their basketball achievements. It is helpful to know what environment you are entering. We will go over things, such as stats and recognition, in a little while.

If you find yourself not being unable to do most things required for your position, don't be discouraged. It is never too late to improve your game. Start working and polishing your skill set today, keep monitoring your progress and stay focused on the task at hand.

<u>Chapter 3</u>
<u>Off the court: Handling your business</u>

Now that you know what kind of player you need to become on the court, let's talk about off the court. There are many factors that will either get you a step closer to your dreams or end them.

You may have heard the term "Student Athlete." Put simply, that is what you're striving to become. The emphasis being on student. Before you can be accepted into college, let alone a scholarship player, you must first become eligible academically. Coaches are not only expecting you to handle business on the court, but also off it too. Academics are an important key to earning extra scholarship money. That's right. You can receive a reduction off your tuition if you meet certain criteria in the classroom. This means you can boost your chances at getting your education as cheap as possible by achieving good grades, as long as you qualify for it.

The Academic Requirements
So what grades do you need to get into college? It varies based on the level of the school athletically and academically. For example, there is a higher focus on academics for a Division I school than a Junior College. How do they measure your academic success? This is calculated using a Grade Point Average system, or GPA. Your GPA is what you obtain in all your subjects on average. For example, a straight-A student would translate to a 4.0 GPA. A student with majority B grades would hover around the 3.0 GPA mark.

For students in the UK, below is a rough converter that will give you an idea of where you're at academically. I'm aware that the grade system has changed for GCSE students, so below is a quick reference if you are one of these students.

UK GCSE Grade	Equivalent
9	A+
8	A
7	A-
6	B+
5	B/ B-
4	C
3	D/ E
2	E/F
1	F/G
U	U

This table will show you where you stand in terms of the US scale of grading.

Grade	Percentage Mark	GPA
A+	≥75	4.25
A	71-74	4.0
A-	67-70	3.75
B+	64-66	3.50
B	61-63	3.25
B-	57-60	3.0
C+	54-56	2.75
C	50-53	2.50
C-	48-49	2.25
D+	43-47	2.0
D	40-42	1.50
D-	38-39	1.0
F+	35-37	0.75
F	30-34	0.5
F-	≤29	0.0

Now let's look at some of the requirements for each level.

If you're aiming to become an NCAA Division I or II player, there are a few more requirements than other levels. The first thing you would need to do is register for a certification account via the NCAA eligibility center. You'll need a valid email address, education history and your sporting participation history for this. The fee for the certification is $90 in the US and Canada. International applicants pay $150. All fees are nonrefundable.

For NAIA basketball, the process is similar, and there will be more information regarding their eligibility process at the end of this book. However, one thing to note is that there are both academic and athletic requirements to be considered eligible. You have to have at least a 2.3 GPA for NCAA DIV I, and at least a 2.2 GPA for NCAA DIV II.

Some schools may be more competitive – like Duke University, for example – and require at least a 4.03 GPA to be considered eligible. If you fall below that, your chances of being accepted are slim. Texas Tech requires at least a 3.57 GPA..
Bottom line: work hard in the classroom.

The other area you need to focus on is with your SATs or ACTs. In order to attend a 4 year university, you must complete the exams within a certain number range, depending on your preferred school's requirements. Both the SAT and ACT require good preparation, as the format is likely something you haven't seen before. The good news is, there are plenty of resources available for you to get the tools you need to do well. I would highly recommend you consider taking your first test during your junior year (age 16-17). You can take the test multiple times, if needed, so you'll be able to better your score before your last year of high school. Both exams are expensive, so you'll want to be as ready as you can be. As a helpful hint: the lower your GPA, the higher your test scores need to be.

The Athletic Requirements
Now for the athletic requirements. Have you ever heard the term, "amateurism?" It's very important to know, and is often a factor why many are not eligible for NCAA sports.

There are a number of ways you can avoid looking like an amateur in the eyes of the NCAA. One of them is by signing a contract. This is a big issue if you are hoping to play college sports. There are some high school kids in Europe who end up being a part of a professional set up, or even choose to take a professional route, as opposed to going directly to college. The main determining factor for these players is whether or not they signed a professional contract and had a paid salary while participating for that team. College hopefuls are also not allowed to have any financial assistance for playing and can't be represented by an agent. Only high school players that are labelled "elite senior prospects" can sign with NCAA certified agents. If you're a player who is able to be a part of a professional team, just ensure you don't sign any contracts or receive any money from the club if you want to keep your college eligibility.

As individuals, we all learn at different rates. Some faster than others. If you feel that you're struggling with certain topics or subjects, don't be too hard on yourself. The most important thing is to identify your weaknesses and work towards strengthening them. Your teachers are there to help and offer support, so don't feel ashamed or embarrassed to approach them if you find something difficult. Outside of school, there are also tutors available who specialise in specific subjects -- English, Mathematics, Science, History, etc. Whatever subject or subjects you struggle in, don't hesitate to work with a tutor. It's also a good idea to take the initiative and use your resources from home. There is plenty of information on the Internet that can help guide you. One website that I found particularly helpful is www.khanacademy.org Here you can find easy explanations for different concepts you might not understand. But the important thing is to start being proactive. As soon as you do this, you will see your life start to change. Be the best student you can be. Don't be an amateur.

On Court and Off Court Performance Let's talk about certain things you can do off the court that will translate to better on court performance. The first thing a coach will look at when considering you to be a part of their roster is your frame. You have to look the part and be in peak athletic shape. Basketball is an up tempo, fast-paced sport, so being in good condition is not only a requirement, but can also give you an edge on the court. The things you do in practice alone will not fully prepare you for college basketball. Sure, the "suicides" and "backboard touches" and anything else your coach has in mind for punishment will help to an extent, but only so much. It is important you develop good habits from a young age, so that these can be a part of your routine and discipline going forward.

One of the most common myths is you need a fitness facility (gym) to improve your athletic performance. If you have one that you can regularly attend, great. But it isn't required. You can do fitness from anywhere. So, if you don't have access to a treadmill, squat rack or bench press – don't skip out on your workout. Find items around your house that you can use to still get it done. Remember, hard work pays off.

Basketball uses all parts of the body, so it's important to have a balanced workout routine. Start with fitness and conditioning. Many coaches encourage running long distance to improve your cardio, but I'm not a huge fan of this. If you think about it, the game of basketball never involves running at the same speed for a prolonged period of time. It involves short quick spurts. That said, it would make more sense to work on sprints. I would recommend working on sprints 3 times a week. The distance should be roughly 50 meters and you should complete 15-20 sets with sufficient rest of 2-3 mins between each set. The key thing is to exert as much energy in each sprint. Sprinting is not only great for improving speed, but it also targets fat loss and improves your explosiveness. All of these will benefit you greatly on the court.

What if it's raining outside and you can't leave your house, do you still workout? Absolutely! No matter the weather – rain or shine – your answer should always be yes. There are plenty of things you can do at home that will help you on the court. One workout I like to recommend to players is what I like to call "the 300 workout." It involves you doing a total of 100 pushups, 100 sit ups and 100 bodyweight squats. This may sound daunting, but not to worry. If you can't do that many, start off with 20 of each and work your way up. The key thing in anything is progression. This workout should be done 3 times a week. After 3-4 weeks of consistently doing this, you should see a difference in your strength, explosiveness and ability to move on the court. Doing this will take your game to another level.

Breakfast of Champions
"You are what you eat," so the saying goes. The greatest challenge many young athletes face is maintaining a good diet. Believe me, what you put in your body has a massive effect on your game. I didn't see the benefits of eating right until later on. I ate so much fast food during my earlier teenage years. I figured that I would burn it all off when working out, but this proved to be costly. I was holding myself back from reaching another level. Your diet can really cancel out the work you put in, so remember this before eating a burger after practice.

Breakfast is vital for all athletes and it is, indeed, the most important meal of the day. It provides the fuel to kick start your day, so having things such as oats or eggs are some good food items to start with. Fruits and veggies should always be a part of your diet, and you should opt for fruits as your snacks as ones that are high in salt and sugar.

Water needs to be your best friend -- I can't stress that enough. A lot of people make the mistake of only drinking water when they are tired during practice. But you need to be well hydrated throughout your day – before, during and after practice. When you sweat, you lose water so you need to have plenty. It can also help prevent cramping.

Your lunches and dinners should have a combination of carbohydrates and protein. Brown rice and pasta are good sources of carbs, and you can get your protein source from chicken and beef. But watch your portion sizes. Everything in moderation. Too much can be counterproductive as you may feel heavier on the court. Other great protein sources include, but are limited to: fish, eggs, lentils and chickpeas. If you are working hard, it is important you are eating enough to not only help you play at your peak, but also your recovery.

Rest
Working hard is a must but something that is just as important is rest! It is important to listen to your body. Overworking can be counterproductive so make sure you take time to recover if you are nursing an injury. One thing that shouldn't be compromised is sleep. Not many teenagers are fond of sleep, but it is one of the biggest contributors to on court success. Sleep is helpful both for the body and the mind. It helps you to think sharper and improve your awareness on the court. Lack of sleep will make you feel lethargic and lazy, which, ultimately, affects your performance.
The separation is in the preparation. If you don't already have these good habits, not to fear. It's not too late. Developing good habits goes a long way and can determine how far you excel in the sport.

Be a Student of the Game
The last athletic requirement is being a student of the game. This really sets aside the elite from the good and the good from the average. The game of basketball is 70% mental. Being able to see a play before it develops is something all great players can do. The ability to do this comes from studying the game on a consistent basis. Coaches not only love players with a high IQ, but also need players with a high IQ in order to be successful. You should aspire to be an extension of the coach on the court.

What does it mean to have a high IQ? For starters, it's not something that happens overnight. It comes with experience. When you play the game, your understanding should naturally progress, through things that are done well and things that fail. However, it goes beyond that as well. Reviewing your game should enable you to see where you went wrong and how to correct it. Be sure to make the most of your available resources, beyond just your coaches and mentors.

We live in an era where we have access to so much information. It's time to make the most of this. You can find most things on Google and YouTube. It's a good idea to watch videos that are specific to the position you play. If you are a point guard, watch players who know how to make good reads, use the pick and roll well and make their teammates better. This will help with how you think about the game. If you're a shooting guard, watch players who move well off the ball and have a quick release. If you're a centre, watch players who are good at defending pick and rolls, switching onto guards and finishing under the basket. Your work should never stop when practice finishes, you should utilise every opportunity to get better. This is not something that you should do occasionally. You need to incorporate these habits into your lifestyle so it becomes a part of who you are.

Chapter 4
The Recruitment Process: Selling yourself

When I was in high school, I made a decision that I wasn't going to wait for an opportunity to come to me. I went out there looking for it. I can't tell you how many hours I spent writing emails and calling coaches trying to get that scholarship offer. The lack of responses were disheartening, but, at the time, I didn't know why. I wasn't sure if it was because of my email, my game film or the school itself. In reality, it was a combination of all three. If I knew what I now know, my approach would have been completely different.

If you are in a similar boat, don't worry. No response is not the end of the world. Being proactive is good! You are taking control of your situation. Let's explore what you may be doing wrong. It's not enough just to reach out to schools, there should be a method with how you contact coaches.

Put yourself into the mindset of a coach. You're extremely busy with preparing for the season. It's pre-season and you're trying to find a winning formula for your team to be successful. You're working long hours and spending a lot of time outside of work watching films on what your team is doing well and where they need to improve. In your free time, you go through a bunch of emails -- mostly those of aspiring high school kids who, like yourself, are trying to get noticed. Coaches receive hundreds to thousands of emails. Especially at the higher levels. So, already you can see two things. First, you have to stand out. Second, you don't have much time to make a good impression. The process of getting noticed is an extensive one, but I'm going to give you some tips and pointers that should steer you in the right direction.

It makes a difference if your coach sends out the email as opposed to the player. It doesn't mean as a player you will never hear back from a coach. It just means that schools have a certain structure they like to follow. They would prefer to keep a dialogue with your coach, as they believe that would be a less biased point of view and they'd be able to ask them more questions about yourself. If you aren't able to rely on your coaches to reach out to schools for you, this means you need to know what college coaches look for when recruiting.

Before even getting to the email stage, it is mandatory that you have game footage ready and available to show to coaches. You can list all your stats and achievements, but, ultimately, what matters to coaches is what you can do to help their program. Your game footage is crucial in getting a response back. Your footage should be a good indicator of how you play and that you're capable of joining the level you're reaching out to. Chapter 2 gave you a good idea of where you stand with that.

Basic Requirements for Your Highlight Reel

1) Quality
Quality is essential. At minimum, your video should be clear and you should be easy to identify. I cannot tell you how many times I look at game film and can't make it through the first minute. I have seen a lot of game tapes where I can't tell which player the mix is for, or, when I'm trying to focus on a specific area of the video, there is too much going on to even see what the player is trying to showcase. College coaches have a lot less patience than myself.

So, make sure your highlight tape is no longer than 5 mins. Preferably between the 2-3 min mark. In the first minute, showcase the best parts of your game. If you're athletic, include these plays in the very beginning. If you're a shooter, highlight your catch and shoot and off the dribble shots early on. As much as coaches love hard-nosed defensive players, college coaches have less patience than myself. They don't have enough time to watch thousands of long, low-quality videos.

2) Special Effects & Soundtrack
Many hopeful players want to make their films look flashy and eye-catching. They put in a minute long introduction. Don't. Leave all black and white special effects, slow motion or long speeches OUT. That shows that you're artistic, not a good basketball player candidate. Same with music. Coaches are not interested in any of this. If you must put in music, though, choose an instrumental track that won't take away from you. No songs with lyrics – especially those that include curse words. That's an automatic no.

Only show your best game play, so coaches want to see and know more.

Are you coachable?
This question will always come up when a coach is recruiting a player. Being coachable isn't just listening to instructions from your coach. It means also being able to implement what you have been told in practices and games. How do you react to criticism? How is your body language? How do you respond in the face of adversity? All this and more your future will want to know.

Being coachable says a lot about you both as a person and as a player. They want to know who you are and will assess things including, but not limited to: your character, how you act in school and if you make an impact in the community. You do not want a bad reputation. Stay out of trouble. Don't be naive and think they won't know. Coaches ask for many references before even beginning the recruiting process, so it is important that you do not have a bad image.

Social media -- coaches check this, so be careful what you post. Countless times, scholarships were taken away because of something a student posted on their social media accounts. Coaches need players they can trust and rely on. Who will be good team players on the court and role models around campus. If you are active on social media, make sure that your content is not incriminating to your character or the people you are representing.

Reaching Out to Coaches

Getting in touch with coaches shows you're serious about their program and have the ability to be proactive. You can't always wait for the door to be opened. Sometimes, you have to go and smash down that door yourself. Below is a draft email for a potential coach:

Dear Coach (enter last name),

I am writing to you because I have interest in being a part of your program for the (enter year) season. In terms of my game, I am a (enter position) who excels in (enter your strength) & (enter another strength). I am a hardworking individual who will do everything I can to help the team's success.

Below is more information on myself and a link to my highlight tape.

Name:
D.O.B:
Country:
Nationality:
Position:
Height:
Weight:
GPA:
Season Averages:
Current Team:

(enter link to highlight footage)

Please let me know if you require a coach's reference or my transcripts. I hope to hear from you soon.
Kind Regards

(enter full name)

So as you can see, the email does not need to be extremely long, but it's very direct and straight to the point. The bio makes it clear for coaches to get the necessary information they require. Make sure that your attached highlight tape is easy to access. Upload it to YouTube if you can.

The other method of communicating with a coach is via phone call. This may be slightly more daunting, but it's nothing that should scare you. If anything, the coach will be happy that you are showing interest in their program. Just make sure that when you call, you are aware of the basics: the coach's name, the level the school plays, the conference they are in and their track record. This lets the coach know you've done your research and you understand the program. Calling the US internationally can be expensive, but there are plenty of affordable international calling cards. The numbers for the coaches can all be found on the school's staff directory via their website.

Remember that being proactive is the only way you can be sure that you are doing all you can. If you don't get a response, or not the response you were hoping for, do not be discouraged. The recruiting process is something you must be persistent with. A follow up email does not hurt anybody, so it's a good idea to check in with coaches if you don't hear anything after a couple of weeks.

Sometimes you may get an automated response from the school with a link to the application. This does not mean the school is interested in you necessarily; it just shows that they require you to apply as part of the early stage recruiting process. Make sure you have done a detailed research on the school before applying as the applications come with a fee. If a coach messages you back directly, that's a good indication. They may say that they are interested and would like to keep in touch or that they want you to send further information. Maybe a coach may tell you that they are not recruiting for your position. In this case, you should still respond and thank them for their email. You never know what may happen down the line.

Keeping records of your season stats are important for a few reasons. Yes, they will be helpful information to a coach, but it's also good to monitor your progress over the course of the season. Don't only focus on your scoring or assist numbers. Pay close attention to your turnover numbers too. For any position you hope to play in college, coaches would prefer you don't turn the ball over at a high rate. If you can calculate your efficiency and field goal percentage, then this will be useful information as well. You shouldn't play the game of basketball for stats. The aim should always be to do what is necessary to help your team win. That said, stats are another opportunity for coaches to assess if you will be a good fit for their program. So keep a record of these.

When should You Reach out to a Coach?

There is never a time that's necessarily too early, but if you wait until your last year of high school, it may be too late. Coaches like to follow the progress of a player from early on, so consider making the initial contact in your Sophomore year (age 15-16). There is nothing wrong with being ahead of the game. If you have a highlight tape at an even younger age, even better. That can work in your favour, depending on how well you are performing. Coaches may not consider you a legitimate prospect until your Sophomore year, though, as that's typically when they have a pretty good idea of how your career will pan out, your maximum height and things of this nature.

How you spend your holidays and summers can make a big impact on how your recruiting pans out. They say players are made in the off season, which I believe wholeheartedly. This is where you have the most time to work on your craft. Many camps take place in the summer, so use these as an opportunity to work on your game. Use it as a measuring tool. See how far your game has come and how far it needs to go. If your goal is to get a scholarship, then your summer can not be wasted. The summer time is also where many competitions and tournaments take place. If you're one of the players in contention to make national team selection, do what you can to be part of the selected 12. If you're a player who isn't in contention, then make it a goal for the following summer. The international tournaments are a great place to gain extra exposure and test yourself against the best in the world. College coaches pay close attention to these events, as it is a great opportunity to see how you perform on the highest stage. One good game or one good tournament can really open doors to your college recruiting.

One such platform to gain more exposure is the Amateur Athletic Union (AAU). This takes place in the United States starting around April then carries throughout the whole summer. College coaches always pay attention to these events as they're able to determine best high school players all at the same time. If you have the opportunity to be a part of an AAU team, you should certainly consider it if it's affordable and feasible for your family.

A number of UK kids go out there and end up finding it a frustrating experience because they aren't given opportunities to showcase what they can do to coaches. For this reason, I have to stress the importance of making sure you're ready before you go there. Assess the situation to see if it's likely you will get an opportunity to show what you're all about. The biggest and most important thing is confidence. Yes, of course, having the necessary skills is a must, but, without confidence, you will not be able to put your skills on display. Coaches will not recruit a player who doesn't believe in themselves.

Some of the more well-known circuits include the Nike EYBL Circuit and the Adidas Gauntlet. If you are able to play for any teams that participate in either of these, I recommend it. Teams that are part of these travel up and down the US, facing opposition from the top high school kids where top college programs attend. There is a serious chance you can get recruited after one day, depending on how you perform. Remember that it is only beneficial to your recruitment if you find a team where you'll have the opportunity to play and showcase your capabilities. These tournaments will do nothing for you if you are stuck on the bench.

Finding the Right Fit
Picture this. You receive your first scholarship offer. A coach tells you that he'd love to have you on the team. All that hard work. Those countless hours you spent in the gym have paid off! If you're part of the small percentage that receives multiple offers, this is where it gets tricky. The most important part of any recruitment process is finding the right fit. I cannot stress this enough. This should be the most important area to address if you hope to have a successful college career.

When choosing a school, it is important to know what you're looking for. Do you have a good relationship with the head coach? This will affect your experience and how you develop as a player. You want the coach to have your best interest at heart, a coach who sees you as a player and a person. They need to be aware of your strengths and weaknesses so they can help guide you towards your goals.

The next thing in choosing the right fit is assessing what your goals are for the season. Everyone may have their own answer to this. For instance, Freshman are rarely expected to be big contributors as opposed to those who are hoping to make an impact from the first year to graduation. So, if you plan to get playing time in your first season, be sure to discuss that with your coach. There are no guarantees, of course, but it's important to know where the coach has you in their plans and if you're willing to earn your spot.

You should do as much research on the school beforehand. On the court, what style of basketball do they play? Do they have much success? What type of players do they recruit? Each one of these things should prove to be a good indicator of where you will fit in the coach's plan. Then, off the court, pay attention to their ideals about academics. How the college is regarded and life after college sports. These are important as the vast majority of students enrol with the intention to graduate. So, be sure not to focus on the basketball side of things alone. You want to find a school that you can call home for your college career. You don't want to rush this decision. Take time to learn about every school and speak with every coach who is recruiting you. Do not dismiss any school immediately. Keep your options open. Each coach has taken their time to reach out, which is a big compliment in of itself. The least you could do is hear what they have to say, consider and then make a decision from there.

High School
There is never such a thing as being too prepared for anything. When players ask me is it ever too early to start planning for your future, I simply respond no. There is always something you can do to be ahead of the pack. When we think about the factors of getting a scholarship, one of the main things that is always talked about is exposure. It's one thing to play well, but if you're not in a situation where you can get noticed, it won't mean much.

High school basketball in the US is the easiest way for college coaches to assess the talent available. It's a level playing field and easy for them to filter out who's a college player and who isn't. One disadvantage of being an international prospect is a lack of eyes and a lack of attention. Unless you're one of the top 3 players in your country for your age group, there is a high chance nobody really knows your name. That is why it is becoming more common for international kids opting to transfer to a US High School as early as 14 or 15 years old. Being seen is important. When you attend high school, you can be assured that good performances will, at least, get some sort of recognition. That may be in the form of local rankings or, depending on the school you go to, national attention.

There are 2 important things to pay attention to if considering going to a high school. One, the level of basketball the school plays. You want to make sure you are playing what they call "Varsity basketball." Varsity is the highest level each school offers and is the only level that college coaches focus on. Second, Junior Varsity. Depending on the school, this may still be a high level of basketball, but typically top colleges don't recruit Junior Varsity players. Make it a goal to be playing Varsity level by Junior year at the latest to give yourself the best shot of landing a scholarship. If you can do it earlier, all the better. With some of the elite programs, it's extremely difficult to have an opportunity to make the Varsity roster, because they recruit top ranked high school kids every year.

Another great thing to consider about a high school is how well known they are. Although going to a recognised school can come with its challenges, you do not want to go to a program where you will struggle to gain much exposure. Some of the smaller schools don't get much attention on a national scale, because they either have a poor record as a school or they've lacked talent. If this is the case, it would be best to look at a different high school.

I've always believed that it takes one moment, one opportunity, one situation for your life to change. If you happen to attend a smaller school but, on the schedule, they face some of the higher ranked programs, it's a great opportunity for you to be seen. There is a high chance that colleges will attend to watch for prospects during the games. If you happen to have a good game, you could catch the eye of a coach, even if they weren't originally looking at you. One good game and you are immediately on the radar. This is something that will not be possible if you aren't playing in the US. Coaches won't travel abroad to watch a prospect they have never heard of.

In high school, you never know who is watching your games, so it's important to bring it every single game. If you are an international player, high school is an avenue that should be considered as young as 13 years of age. Do your research, reach out to schools, talk to coaches and get as much information as possible. It could be just what you need in terms of getting used to the US style of play and boost your chances of earning a scholarship.

Prep Basketball

Prep basketball -- often referred to as post graduate basketball -- is the ultimate springboard for any athlete considering college basketball. When I was in the 10th grade (15-16 years of age), I had a goal that, after my last 2 years of high school education, I would then be ready to make the transition to college basketball. Two years seem like a long enough time to prepare for this, but it all depends on the stage of development you are at. The following year, I quickly realised that, to even have a chance at making a college roster, I would need a prep year. Many international players choose to do a prep season in the US before college for a number of reasons, but mainly to get used to the US style of basketball and get extra exposure from colleges.

The "prep" in Prep basketball is short for "preparatory." It is intended to prepare you for college, not just on the court but off the court too. There are many prep schools in the US, many of which have a strong basketball program. A large majority of the top high school teams also have a prep program and produce a high number of college prospects year in and year out. The amount of lessons I learned during my prep year I still apply to this very day. I actually attended 2 schools within that 1 year, and it was a testing year for me.

Being in a prep school taught me that success does not come without sacrifice and discipline. We had to be up early for school; after school we would have practice. Straight after that, I would finish up homework and have dinner. This was the usual routine every day, but there was a turning point for me early in that season. I had to ask myself if I was really doing enough to be the best player I could be or if I was just following structure. I then decided to wake up an hour early to make sure I could get at least 30 mins of hoops before school started. After dinner, I would make sure I did some form of conditioning – mainly jump rope -- before going to bed.

Prep school really helped me develop good habits that progressed my career. The most beneficial aspect of Prep basketball for me, however, was the basketball schedule. The schedule itself was very tough, but it is what every high school kid hoping to play college needs. We not only faced some of the best Prep programs in the area, but also played against nationally ranked Junior Colleges and faced off against NAIA schools. The schedule is set out intentionally to see how you fair against college teams. It's a good indicator for you and for coaches looking to recruit.

There were many eye-opening games for me when faced up against college teams that was my real introduction to US basketball. Not only was it a lot faster than what I was used to, but you're going up against big time athletes who have a much bigger frame than most high school players. Our team at times felt out of our depth when faced with some of the ranked Jucos.

I remember facing the number 2 ranked Junior College -- Trinity Valley. This soon turned out to be a game to forget for our team. I'm pretty sure they had double digit dunks in the opening 5 mins. After every score, they would make it extremely difficult for our team to get over our half. It really showed me what to expect if I ever wanted to play college ball. Everything they did was 5x more intense and aggressive.

Now prep schools can be quite costly for international students, but there are many that offer scholarships to attend. The relationships you build, the adversity you face, the experience you gain from travelling up & down the US -- all are things, cherish them. It will only get you better prepared to play college hoops, and is essentially a rehearsal for when you start college. Staying on top of your school work with a busy basketball schedule, being self-dependent and developing responsibility. Not folding under pressure on the biggest stage -- this is what you need to get accustomed to. There's no better place than a prep program.

Like choosing a college, choosing a suitable prep school is equally important. You do not want to waste a year, by any means, so there are a few things to consider. First, is it affordable? Many prep schools cost the same amount or higher than a year's worth of college tuition. Don't get me wrong. Many programs do offer state of the art facilities, world class training and needed exposure, but it can be hard to justify the price tag. You never really want to spend more than what you may be expected to pay for your college tuition. It's important to ask yourself: why do you want to go to a particular program? Is the sole focus to develop as a player and a person, or is it perhaps the experience of living in a different culture and environment? Is it strictly to get exposure for college?

Second, do as much research as you can about the programme. What is the school's recent success like? What type of players do they produce? How many kids have they sent to college on scholarship? These are key for you to see if a programme matches with what you're looking for. I would also find out the living arrangements and meal plans they have for the players. If you're expecting a glamorous 5 star service at a prep programme, you may be in for a rude awakening. There are many that have respectable arrangements for living and providing meals for the players. If you're lucky, you may have a set up with a host family that treats you well. Then there are those, however, that do the bare minimum in regards of lifestyle. Expect dorms, bunk beds and a lot of frozen foods as your meals. It's unlikely it will be a terrible living situation, but make sure you are aware of the accommodations before deciding to avoid any disappointment.

Third, and perhaps the most important thing, is your relationship with the coach. This will determine if it's even worth attending the programme. Make sure you get to know the coach. For many, a prep year will be viewed as almost a last chance to make their college dreams come true. So, it is important that you spend time building a good relationship with the coach before choosing your destination. At the end of the day, the coach you play for will have major implications on how schools recruit you and how much exposure you get. When colleges are recruiting, the point of reference is what the other players say about the coach.

All in all, Prep basketball was an experience that changed my life on and off the court. It was the first real taste of adversity I had faced. Sure, I have had my fair share of disappointment playing the game, but it is completely different when you are thousands of miles away from home. Being on the other side of the world meant that I had no choice but to learn responsibility and accountability. So often, we get too comfortable in a situation and become self-reliant on others. I believe everyone, at some point in their lives, needs to be challenged, especially if they are striving to achieve something great. Challenges are self-defining moments. They reveal a lot about who you are individually. From a basketball perspective, Prep basketball was everything I needed. It clearly gave me a much needed reality check.

Playing against a much higher level of competition will force you to adjust your game and adapt. You may be a point guard and feel you have a great handle. How do you know that if you haven't played against the best on ball defenders? You might believe you can make it as a shooter at the college level, but can you keep your cool when being closed out by an athletic 6'8 wing? The prep circuit is a great way for you to find out if you're ready for college ball. If you can make it work, I would strongly recommend it.

Transferring
So, you weren't able to land a scholarship to the US after your last year of high school. It's your first week of university in the UK and you're wondering if it's too late to keep your college hoop dreams alive. The dream is not over, but it may be a little tougher. Because you're no longer going to enter college as a Freshman, the expectations are different. When colleges recruit Freshmen, the expectations are for them to learn the first couple of years and then be big contributing factors from the end of Sophomore year to the beginning of Junior year. There are some exceptions, usually with the bigger name schools. A lot of these schools recruit many Freshmen to start in their first year. The most competitive schools in the NCAA have many Freshmen leave to enter the NBA draft after 1 season.

With all schools, whether your goal is to play NCAA or NAIA, transfers need to be prepared to make an impact right away. A good place to start is knowing how many years of eligibility you have remaining. This can be quite complicated as different levels have different rules. Your eligibility is not based on age, but the period of time that you graduated high school. For UK kids, this is typically year 13, or, in some cases, an additional year due to a course change. Every player has what they call your "college clock." This starts ticking usually once you've graduated.

Let's breakdown the eligibility rules surrounding the NCAA & NAIA.

NCAA
Division I: As mentioned previously, you have a 5 year window to compete for 4 years. The clock only starts, however, when you enrol as a full-time student at any university/college. The key thing to note is full time and the NCAA defines this as being enrolled in 12-hour credits in a term. Check with not only the university you are studying at, but also the school you hope to transfer into to confirm how many credits your course is worth.

The extra year is what they refer to as a "grace period." This may mean you choose to redshirt for the year. In other words, you won't be expected to play that season due to lack of readiness or possibly injury, but will still be involved in team activities. Once your clock begins, it continues regardless of situation or circumstance. Some players do not enrol in full-time college education immediately after high school, so their clock doesn't start until they do.

Division II & III: For Division II & III, it may be a little trickier to understand. They measure your eligibility clock in semesters once you've enrolled as a full-time student. Instead of years, they give you 10 semesters to finish your 4 years of competition. With semesters – or terms – you have two per year, Spring and Fall. The only time a semester is counted is if you are enrolled full-time, regardless of competition, or you are a part-time student who has participated in competition for the school. The same redshirt rules apply for these divisions.

NAIA: If you're hoping to transfer to an NAIA, it's important to know that the rules are slightly different. You cannot participate in the NAIA until 16 weeks after your last sporting competition. If you plan to transfer half-way through the season, you must receive what they call a "release letter" from your current institution's athletic department, enabling you to move on from the programme. If you do plan to take this route, ensure your grades are respectable, as you're required a minimum of a 2.0 GPA, to do this, as well as any further requirements your desired school needs. You must also complete a total of 24 semester credit hours within the last 2 semesters. So, on average, 12 per semester, but must be a total of 24.

NJCAA: The transfer rules for the NJCAA or community colleges are slightly different to the NAIA. If you have completed one term as a full-time college student, you must have completed 12 credit hours with a GPA of 1.75 or higher. If you have completed two terms, you must still have 12 credit hours completed with a 2.0 minimum GPA. Be sure you know how all the levels affect your college clock.

So whether you are thinking of transferring to a US high school, prep school or college, make sure you give it some serious thought. Change, at any point, will have massive implications on how your career pans out, so make sure each move is calculated. Do your research, learn about what each school has to offer and see which school will allow you to evolve into the best version of yourself.

Chapter 6:
Support System & Mindset

They say your circle is a representation of who you are. Who are the types of people that you are around the most? Who are the people you are most invested in? Are the people in your circle helping you progress, or are they holding you back? Is your circle full of winners and hard workers or those who are lazy and have a negative mindset? People often feel they can influence everyone around them but don't see the danger of having people around them who affect their way of thinking negatively. Now, it's not always obvious, but slowly you see yourself skipping one practice or taking shortcuts in workouts. I experienced this myself. The greatest years of my development happened when I was around people better than me and more experienced than myself. If they saw me showing any sign that I was about to quit, they would keep me in check. If they saw me content with a decent performance, they would remind me that there is more work to be done.

You need people around you who support you and hold you accountable. The worst thing you can do for someone you care about is lie to them. I'm referring, specifically, to progress. When I made a mistake, I would want the people around me to point it out because it meant that I had an opportunity to learn from it. These are the same people who would notice when I made progress too, so it works hand-in-hand. You can't control who is around you all the time as you progress in the sport. You will meet a lot of different people, and this includes new coaches and new teammates. All these people have some sort of influence over the player you turn out to be. It is always helpful when your coach and family is supportive, and teammates are encouraging your goal. But what happens when they aren't? How will you adapt to this type of situation? Will you be able to adjust to this environment?

At some point in your career, you will be faced with a scenario where you're not seeing eye to eye with your coach or teammates. You should never let this affect what you're trying to achieve. You should still be the hardest worker you can be, still be the best teammate you can be and not lose sight of the end goal. The journey is not always swift. It can certainly feel rocky at times, but it is important you do not let the situation change you. You must focus on controlling what you can control. Like the friends we hang out with and spend time with. You should be smart enough to identify which friends have a good influence over your goals and which do not. It is important to identify this early, as it can play a role in how quickly you recover from a setback and how motivated you will become to keep on performing at a high level.

Self-Belief
"The man who says he can and the man who says he can't are both correct." This is one of my favourite quotes from the Chinese philosopher, Confucius. I want you to think about this quote for a moment. What are your thoughts on it?

As individuals, when faced with a task or opportunity, we all have a choice. A way to approach it. At the start of the book, we touched on seeing something to believe it. I stand by this 100%. In order to make your dreams a reality, you must believe it's possible. If you can develop your mind to see what can work and what can't, you start to break the limitations in your life. This could be in anything, on the court or in the classroom. Many people are so quick to see a challenge and immediately count themselves out. They don't imagine a reality where they see themselves in that position. They say thoughts become things, and how you think really goes a long way to achieving this. If you don't believe you can do something, you have already failed. Seeing the glass half full instead of half empty will determine how you approach and react to adversity.

In order to deal with adversity, you need a strong will and a determined spirit. Everyone faces adversity at some point in their lives, but it is how you respond that will dictate where you go. Let's look at some common hurdles you may face on your journey. Picture the first day of pre-season again. You are ready to compete and make a good impression on the coach. You're taking care of business on the offensive end and making defensive play after defensive play. Throughout the whole pre-season, the coach says how impressed he is with your play and your approach to the season. Fast forward 3 weeks. The team's list is out. You're feeling confident about your chances of making the first team and check the list. Your name is not on the list for the first team, so you go to have a word with your head coach. The head coach tells you that you have a lot of potential, but are not quite ready for the first team this early into the season. What is going through your mind at this point? How will you react knowing you gave it all those 3 weeks of preseason?

This is something to think about deeply, because how you would respond in this situation will tell a lot about your character and your mindset. There are some people who will see this as the end of the road or accept their situation for what it is. Other people will see this as an opportunity to rise to the occasion and prove people wrong. Life is all about perspective. How you view a situation will play a role in the outcomes. I would hope that you would use a situation like this to your advantage. Use it as fuel and motivation to take your game to new heights. There is a saying, "Be so good they can't ignore you." If you have this mindset and continue to outwork those around you, your time will surely come.

Let's imagine a different scenario, one that is common to many in the world of sports. You are past the midway point in the season and have started to find your rhythm as a team. Not only that, but also you as an individual are playing some of your best basketball in your career. Everything is clicking for you. Your shot has been falling all year long and you feel sharper than ever. Before the season, you viewed this as a breakthrough year and had your sights on making noise in the playoffs. The first round of the playoffs have now arrived, and you're getting your usual pregame butterflies. You know once the whistle blows, it's showtime. The jump ball goes up and you're locked in. Your team comes out of the blocks firing. You start the game, connecting on your first 4 shots; but, on the very next play, you go up for a contested layup and land awkwardly. Immediately, you know something is wrong with your knee. A few days later, you get confirmation that your season is over.

I want you to think about all the emotions and thoughts going through your head at that moment in time. You know everything you invested in -- to be so close to the finish line, then told that you have to restart. It's a tough pill to swallow. One of the hardest things for any player is regaining their rhythm. To have all that momentum destroyed is not easy. With any setback, you have a decision to make. Are you going to accept this as your outcome and leave it at that? Not many people are going to expect you to come back better, stronger and faster. Are you going to prove them right? Maybe you're going to defy the odds and be what they never saw coming. In order to become that, you have to get in your head that you're bigger than anything life throws at you.

It all starts with how you think. Your mind can be your best friend and worst enemy at the same time. A wise man once said, "There are no limitations for those who believe and those who are willing to work for their dream." These limits you believe exist are all in your mind, so try to practice positive thinking. There are going to be many setbacks in your basketball journey, many moments where you are overlooked and doubted. But, one thing you should always remember: you have the power to write your legacy. Do you want to be remembered as someone who quit at the first hurdle? Or do you want to be remembered as the person who never quit? The choice is yours.

Fear is an Illusion
You may have heard many of your favourite motivational speakers talk about fear being an illusion or fear not being real. In some ways, this is very true. Fear is something that we create ourselves. Before looking into the causes of fear, it is important to understand what fear actually is. Fear comes in many forms. It may be due to adversity, doubt or even the unknown. The way we tackle fear is by understanding the reasons we are fearful in the first place. If you are trying to progress in any area of life, the worst thing you could do is to run away from your fears. One of the reasons we fear is often the fear of entering a place of discomfort; but, is this a bad thing. The answer to that is no. In order for you to grow in anything, you must leave your comfort zone. If we look at some of the areas in our lives that scare us, this may start to make more sense for you.

Think of any big task you may have faced already or are going to face. What is your approach? Do you often feel out of your depth or do you try to have an optimistic approach? In your life, there are many challenges and uphill battles that will come your way. Let's keep it real here. Gaining a scholarship is a big thing and is not easy.

I want to pose a question to you. When it comes to your dreams, what scares you the most and why? Think about this. The fear of failure is a common answer. But, what is it about failure that scares you? Don't feel ashamed because this is completely normal. Something people don't realise is that failure is a requirement in order to succeed. Think of any successful person. Anyone you think of has failed many times in their lives. The reason why they are so successful is because they have failed many more times than people have even tried. Failing to do something is always an opportunity to learn from that shortcoming. Michael Jordan even said it himself, "I've missed more than 9000 shots in my career. I've lost almost 300 games. 26 times, I've been trusted to take the game winning shot and missed. I've failed over and over and over again in my life, and that is why I succeed." If Michael Jordan, one of the greatest athletes the world, has ever seen can say this, maybe you need to change your view on failure. So next time there are tryouts for a team that you don't quite feel ready for, just go. Next time a coach asks you to demonstrate a drill, be confident in yourself. When a coach draws up a play for you to take the game winning shot, look your coach confidently in the eye and tell them yes. Without trying, you miss out on valuable experiences, experiences that will shape you and allow you to grow.

So, how do you develop the confidence to go out and perform? Confidence comes from preparation. Fail to prepare, prepare to fail. If you can develop the correct mindset of training, you will always manage to elevate. You need to be your own harshest critic, a mindset where you are never satisfied. This does not mean that you fail to see how far you have come, but instead realise that there is always room to improve. Setting regular goals allows you to keep on track. Once you smash one goal, you set yourself a new goal. Regularly challenging yourself will enable you to not only improve your areas of weaknesses, but also capitalise on the strengths you already have.

When you start to get into a consistent routine and good habits of working hard, you stand a chance against anybody. Simply because you know the work you've put in, you know how much you have sacrificed. Once you understand this concept, fear and pressure do not exist. They are both states of mind. Why is it that some people feel less pressure than others? You're both competing in the same game with the same stakes on the line; but, for some reason, some players feel more nervous than others. This just goes to show that fear can be eliminated, It comes down to 2 main things: your actions and your perspective. They say perception is reality. Your viewpoint of a situation defines the situation. If you view a challenge as achievable or out of your reach, it is going to show in your actions. How you prepare mentally and physically will follow the same mindset you have. Every individual who has gone on to do great things, once upon a time, made a decision. They made a decision to chase their dream with everything they have. If you're not giving it your all, then there really is no point in chasing it at all. Once you start to develop and experience success, set new challenges. Keep yourself hungry to strive for more. Try to break records that have been set, because those are meant to be broken. When you start to think positively, your life around you starts to change.

"I can do this. It can be done."

The words you say are extremely powerful. You need to start realising the impact of what you say. Start having an optimistic approach to things and see what barriers you are able to overcome. There is no guarantee that you will succeed; but, what I can guarantee is, you will never reach a goal if you have no belief.

Goal Setting
Goals are so important. They not only give you something to aim for, but also hold you accountable. Many people talk about setting "S.M.A.R.T" goals, which makes sense, but this sometimes makes people feel that they should put a ceiling on their dreams. I'm all for being ambitious and dreaming big, on the condition that these dreams have a blueprint to them. What necessary steps are you going to take to get to those dreams? When setting an end goal, don't focus on what you can't become. Focus on how great you can become. Once upon a time, the great players you idolise were in the same position as you. Their success did not come without hard work or believing they could make it.

The goals you set will depend on how ambitious you are and will say a lot about how hard you are willing to work. There is no point setting a goal that can be achieved with minimal effort. The whole purpose of setting goals is to want to improve. "Aim for the stars and if you fail, you'll land on the moon."

Let's look at some of the different areas you may cover when preparing for a basketball season. Below is one way of writing down your goals.

Goals

End Goal:

By the end of Summer I want to:

By the beginning of the Season I want to:

By Christmas I want to:

By the end of the Season I want to:

Look at this layout for a list of goals. Although it is a step in the right direction, it is lacking some detail. The late Nelson Mandela once said, "A vision without action is just a dream." I have found this to be very true and, in some instances, I have had to learn the hard way. Anyone can claim they want to accomplish or achieve something; but, until you actually take that first step towards it, it becomes pointless. It's not only important to set goals, but to also keep track of them on a consistent basis. That way you can see if you are making progress towards your goals. In order for you to reach your long term goals, you cannot rely on only team practices, work will need to be done outside of it.

Below is a table for you to monitor your progress each week. The focus is keeping some of your core fundamentals sharp throughout the season and requires you to do so in your own time for a minimum of 3 times a week. Ideally, you should work on these things every day, but 3 times a week outside of practice times is a good place to begin. Note that it not only asks you to record the attempts you take but the makes too, therefore, giving you a percentage. You have all heard the saying, "Train smarter not harder." Calculating your percentage each week allows you to set a benchmark for your goals. You will be able to clearly identify if you are progressing, regressing or staying the same. Some drills will be easier to complete if done with a partner. This will be great for motivating each other and creating a healthy competitive environment. This does not mean you shouldn't work out if you don't have a partner. Sure, you're going to have to chase extra rebounds, but guess what? Make progress not excuses. Find a way to get better.

Week	Day 1			Day 2			Day 3		
Goals	Attempts	Makes	%	Attempts	Makes	%	Attempts	Makes	%
25 right hand layups									
25 left hand layups									
25 reverse right hand lay ups									
25 reverse left hand layups									
10 catch & shoot mid range right corner									
10 catch & shoot mid range middle									
10 catch & shoot mid range left corner									
10 catch & shoot 3's right corner									
10 catch & shoot 3's middle									
10 catch & shoot 3's left corner									

As you can see, each goal gives you a window to achieve it by. Please note that the end goal will be at the top of the page, so it can serve as a reminder of what you're working towards and should act as motivation for you to stay on track.

They say if your goals don't scare you, then you're not dreaming big enough. Set a goal to be one of the top 5 players, shooters or defenders in your league. Aim to be considered for national team selection. Why stop there? Aim to make the team and become an important member of the team. You are only confined by the walls you build yourself, so don't sell your dreams short.

What do you do if certain circumstances prevent you from achieving goals, such as falling out of favour with a coach or perhaps injuries? These are all very common scenarios and situations you may face more than once in your basketball journey. I want you to remember something. Failing to achieve a goal does not make you a failure. You always have a chance to correct your shortcomings. You have the power to write your story. Use a setback as motivation to achieve more. All the pain and disappointment you felt when you came up short, don't ignore those feelings. You should instead use that as fuel to not be in that position again. You can only control what you can control. Remember what it felt like to fail, but don't dwell on it. We can't change the past, but we can change our future.

A Winning Mentality
What do you define as a winning mentality? Would you say that it's simply a desire to win or enjoy winning? Is it a mentality to win at all costs, regardless of how you get there? Or maybe it's having such a fear of failure that you losing is simply not an option. Whichever side you're on, one thing is for sure. People do not get to the top without having some type of winning mentality.

Growing up, a winning mentality was not always there for me. It would depend on the day. Some days I would want to win. Other days, not so much. I had the mindset that "tomorrow is a new day." This is not necessarily a bad mindset, but it certainly had a negative impact on my performance. It only really changed when I played for one coach in the Dallas area. Here, I showed competitive fire, but it had an on and off switch. This coach, to this day, is the craziest coach I have met.

If you show any signs of weakness, or display anything that resembles a losing mentality, he will let you hear it. He did not believe in "coasting" or "kind of working hard". If you were going to do something, you would have to do it with intensity. The way I carried myself mattered to him -- posture, mannerisms, everything. If we were playing a friendly pick up game, there was nothing friendly about it whether he was coaching or playing. He emphasised the importance of competing in everything you do, which meant both on and off the court. During that difficult period in my life, I fell out of love with the sport and was at a crossroads with if I wanted to carry on. He really made me question my passion and love for the game, and I had to ask myself if I'm a quitter. It was the hardest 3 months of my life, but it shaped who I became. I wish I had had a coach like him 3 years earlier.

Winners are not born, they are bred. You always have 2 choices when it comes to doing something. You can take part or take over. This goes back to realising your "why." Are you simply on the court to make numbers, or is it deeper than that? Are you content with giving 50, 70 or 90% of your effort to help your team win? Does it bother you at all when you lose a game, regardless of what is at stake? These are all questions you should think about and ask yourself. 50% of a game is decided before you even step on the court. From the first whistle, you can always see who's up for the battle. The 50/50 balls, the extra rebounds, the intensity levels heading into the last quarter. All of these things can decide who wins a game, but it all starts with the mentality. We're going to talk more about this in the next chapter and the importance of having a competitive nature.

Chapter 8
Networking: Who you know

We have talked about the importance of being proactive in this book, and, no doubt, it is an important aspect in you gaining a scholarship. Being proactive doesn't necessarily mean you have to do everything alone. Getting as much help as possible will only boost your chances. Who you know will play a big role in your recruitment, so I cannot stress the importance of networking enough. From coaches to scouts, all the way down to parents, you may meet someone who can steer you in the right direction. I'm going to give you a brief example surrounding my current life that shows how networking can open doors.

When I was studying in college, it never really crossed my mind that I would be doing anything in the sports recruiting field. One thing I did do was make meaningful relationships with coaches and teammates over the years. Last December, I went to visit a player I had sent out to a high school in Seattle for his opening game of the season. His head coach mentored me in Texas. The relationship I had with the head coach is what enabled me to help another kid many years later down the line. A lesson you should take from this is, you never know how far one conversation can go. When you're at a camp or clinic, take time to talk to different coaches. Ask questions. Be inquisitive. Most importantly, don't be afraid to tell them your goals and dreams. Coaches love to see ambitious kids who want to reach the top. This will not come across the wrong way. If anything, they will be more willing to help you since you took the time and made the effort to talk to them. That one introduction you gave can likely leave a long lasting impression, which can then lead them to introducing you to a coach or a scout in the US. The worst thing that will come out of a situation like this is you gaining more information. That one moment may be a key difference maker. How you approach the game on the court and off the court may change because of some insight you received.

There are many kids who all have the same dream, but there are a number of reasons why they're unable to earn a scholarship. I decided to interview a number of players who once had dreams of heading to the US, some still play the game and some do not. Everyone had a slightly different path, but, from their answers, you'll see some of the same barriers that came up in their journey.

The main questions I asked were:

- What do you think were the biggest influences in you not being able to achieve a scholarship?
- What could you have done differently to give you a better chance to earn a scholarship?

Person A: "I would say the biggest reason I wasn't able to earn a scholarship to the US was the timing in which I did things. Specifically speaking, reaching out to schools. I left it quite late and it wasn't until the end of my Senior year in high school that I started getting in contact with schools. By this time, schools were telling me that they were unable to give me a full scholarship as it was so late into the year. I tried to get some help from coaches here in the UK, but it was a bit last minute. I always felt I was good enough to compete out in the US, but I wasn't knowledgeable about the process or how things worked in general. If I could do things again, I would have started the recruitment process much sooner."

Person B: "I feel the main reason I didn't end up in the US was the path I chose. I was very serious about playing basketball and trying to progress, but my choice of sixth form meant I wasn't exposed to higher levels of basketball. I was only playing competitively outside of school, but, had I attended an academy, I would have had a better level of training and been in a situation to get noticed more. My coach at the time did have some connections, but I feel choosing to attend an academy would have potentially introduced me to more opportunities to earn a scholarship to the US."

Person C: "I was a late starter to the game of basketball (16/17), but I developed quite quickly. I was even able to make the regional team the following summer for my age group. Many coaches were telling me I had a lot of potential to do something in the sport, and tried to steer me towards attending a basketball academy for my 2 years of sixth form. I chose not to, as I felt the academy option wouldn't benefit my academic aspirations. Although I had coaches encouraging me, I didn't see the pathway to the US being a realistic one for myself. My perception of a scholarship player was possibly different to reality. I had friends who I felt were much better than I was attending NCAA Division II schools. This was still a great achievement, but, to me, I felt that, if I wasn't on their level, then my chances of landing anything were very slim. I was not aware of how many levels there were to play college basketball. If I was to change anything, it would have been starting the game earlier. I feel my confidence in my ability would have been greater and my skill set would have been better to where I could have become a scholarship player."

Now if we look at all these examples, it is evident that they all lacked guidance in some way, shape or form. Whether that be starting the sport earlier or choosing the correct pathway, having someone to advise them early in their journey would have benefitted them.

Person A felt that if they started the process maybe a season earlier, they would have been able to secure a scholarship. But it's possible they didn't have anyone around them to tell them that sooner. Who you meet and who you know can be a big deciding factor in why you fall short of your goals or why you reach them.

Person B believed the biggest reason was the environment they were in played a role as to why they didn't land a scholarship. Sometimes, the people you are around can influence you in ways you don't expect. If you are around hardworking individuals who all have the same goals, naturally you will work harder and have higher standards. Another benefit of being in a more competitive environment, or a more established program, is meeting more knowledgeable people who have gone where you want to go. A school with success is more likely to be well connected with programs in the US, so attending a program like this will only increase your chances.

Person C had a slightly different take overall, but still faced the same challenges. It was not necessarily a lack of opportunities, but a lack of information that led to a different perspective. They felt that they didn't meet the standards to earn a scholarship to the US because they hadn't been playing long enough. If person C had a coach who could identify the potential from a younger age, then, not only would their game have improved, but also their understanding of what scholarship player is would have been better.

These are only 3 examples, but I hope these motivate you to make the most of your resources around you and work on your networking skills. The scholarship process heavily involves the element of marketing yourself. It's almost a sales pitch to a company. The product is yourself and the pitch is the email you send out, which includes your game film and season stats. So use every platform to your advantage. Instagram and Twitter are a few ways in which coaches interact with players. A reminder that these platforms can be used as a tool, but can also negatively impact your chances if you have anything that could be incriminating or detrimental to your character.

Chapter 9:
Student of Life

The walk of life is not the same for everyone. Many face different situations and hardships. The one thing that isn't compromised is our opportunity to learn something new every single day. The ability to learn is a skill, one that will take you far in life, whatever it is that you are chasing. Being able to learn from the people around you will not only help you in your pursuit of getting a scholarship, but also being a better individual period. So often, people are scared to ask questions whether they are embarrassed or feel they are too good to ask certain people things. I'm here to tell you that this particular mindset will only hold you back from reaching the highest level. It is not a sign of weakness to not understand. Rather, thinking you are too good to learn from others, is the real weakness. Coaches constantly talk about how they love players who are coachable, willing to learn and hungry to get better. Being coachable shouldn't be only applicable to on the court, but in life too.

Focus strictly on the basketball court for a moment.

-One common scenario you'll all face is joining a new team. The season is approaching and you are struggling to remember the plays that the coach taught you. Everyone seems to understand what plays are being run each time, but you seem lost. You hold your hand up to ask a question. The other players start laughing, making you feel embarrassed and hesitant to ask anything after that.

The question for you is: how will you respond the next time you don't understand something? It's completely understandable to shy away from asking any more questions. I know. I used to feel this way. But this is actually the opposite of how you should respond.. Here's why. Players don't want to feel like they are incapable of keeping up, especially in an environment such as a basketball team. What you need to realise is two things. One, you were selected to be a part of the team for a reason, the coach identified your value already. Second, the coach will not expect everyone to understand everything right away. Being silent, however, will hurt your team moving forward.

Communication is a big factor in every team's success, so better to ask and learn than to stay quiet and guess. If you feel uncomfortable being vocal in the middle of practice, ask if the coach can explain to you at the end of practice. The coach will be more than happy to go through anything you don't understand, so try to do this earlier rather than later. There is no such thing as a dumb question. Everyone starts somewhere. Once you have an answer to a question, it is then your responsibility to study anything that you are not certain on. Little by little, you will begin to feel more comfortable in practices, which will give you the opportunity to help someone else who was in your position.

There is a term we like to use in basketball called, "Being a sponge." As the name suggests, being able to absorb everything around you. Believe it or not, you can learn something new every time you step onto a basketball court. That can mean learning from teammates, coaches or even yourself. As a player, the daily goal should be to be better than you were yesterday. Don't participate in the session just for the sake of participating. Before each week of practice, you should have your own goals. But, even better, ask your coach what they would like for you to work on in that week. Regularly check in with your coach to ask them for feedback on how you're performing. Your judgement will not be enough. Get an opinion from people more experienced than yourself. That way, you're approaching each practice with a purpose. This should not be limited to just team practices.

When you attend camps, you should be just as inquisitive. The purpose of camps is to get better in one way or another, so, even if you feel you haven't improved physically, you should at least come away from the camp improving mentally. How you view the game and how you think in different in game situations. Don't feel nervous to ask other coaches on areas you can improve. Coaches love helping younger players progress. That short 2 minute conversation could be so impactful to your basketball journey.

If you're fortunate enough to be around pros, ask as many questions as you can. As mentioned earlier in the book, who you know really does play a role in your chances of landing a scholarship. My biggest downfall was failing to connect with the right kind of people, nobody expects you to achieve this alone. If you come into contact with a coach that is well informed about the process, ask questions. If you're in contact with a coach you hope to be a part of their program, don't just showcase yourself but ask for feedback. How can you get better? What can you change in order to be considered a legitimate prospect?

You don't want to be just a student of the game, but a student of life. The people who go the furthest in life are the ones who are the most willing to learn. Once you're able to grasp this, you will see a change in your fortunes.

Chapter 10:
Lights, Camera, Action

Now that you've made it to the last chapter, you should have a better understanding of not only the process of recruiting, but also how to be a better player in general. The world we live in is extremely competitive. Getting a scholarship is no different. With every dream or goal you have, just realise that many others likely have that dream. The biggest determining factor, however, is yourself. How do you become the best possible version of you? How do you need to think? What do you need to do in order to separate yourself from the rest? Every individual who achieves something in life has some sort of competitive edge, some more than others.

People try to label competitiveness as a flaw. This is something I completely disagree with. There is no such thing as caring too much, only caring or not caring. Think of anything you ever tried to accomplish in life. The first thing you had to have was desire. Once you have that, everything else follows -- the hard work, the perseverance, the mindset that you won't quit until you achieve.

Growing up in the UK, the most glaring thing I felt players lacked was the same grit and determination of US basketball players. They really make you earn every single thing on the basketball court and you see this at all levels. Young kids playing with a chip on their shoulder. Until you can develop that competitive nature -- that never die attitude -- you should probably consider pursuing something else. Winners win and losers lose.

I want to leave you with 5 important character traits required for gaining a scholarship. I want you to take note of these things and be able to apply these to not just your life on the court, but also outside of basketball too. These traits should enable you to have any success you so wish to have; but, without them, the dream becomes unachievable.

Desire
Earlier in this book, we talked about the importance of seeing something to believe it. Imagine a reality where you achieve a goal. Success doesn't come without having a want, having a desire. "Who wants it more?" It's so easy to say, Yes, I want it more," but can you show it? Can you consistently prove that you will be the hardest worker in the room at all times? Can you show that your desire to win will be greater than your fear of failure? Can you overcome doubters, haters and naysayers?

Talk is extremely cheap. Prove it. Not to your coaches, peers or family. Prove it to yourself. Back up what you talk about or don't talk at all. The one thing you can be sure of is your work ethic. You won't always be the most gifted player or most skilled, but something that should never be taken away from you is your hunger to excel. You may know an NBA player with the name of Patrick Beverley of the Los Angeles Clippers. If you want to try to understand what being hungry means, just research his story and journey to the NBA. The hardships, the setbacks and the barriers he faced would not have been overcome if it wasn't for his desire. Even just by watching him play, you can tell he has something to prove. His passion for the game is evident every time he steps on the court and is the type of player every coach would love to have. I advise you take a page out of his book and have the same level of intensity every time you step on the court. If you're not going to do something 100%, then don't bother doing it at all.

Preparation

Preparation is the foundation of success. We spoke in great detail about preparation being a necessary component to reaching the top. We, as individuals, all have the same 24 hours in a day. it's only when we correctly utilise our time that those hours then have value. Every decision you make matters if you're trying to achieve something not many people manage to do. From the time you decide to wake up to the time you decide to sleep, you must manage your time wisely. Being organised is an underrated trait, which is not talked about enough. Relying solely on talent will only get you so far. You need to be a few steps ahead or you eventually get left behind. It's never too early to start preparing for your dream. There is never such a thing as being too prepared.

The preparation for success is something that is done on a daily basis. The great Aristotle said, "We are what we repeatedly do; therefore, excellence is not an act but a habit." Being great is not something that is achieved one time or occasionally. It is a part of who you are. When someone is great at what they do, everything they do is with that focus in mind. The mentality, the circle of friends, the approach to their craft. Every single thing in their lives must embody greatness.

Now that you know more about what is required to achieve, there really is no excuse. Research, study and learn the game as much as you can. At the end of the day, if you fall short, then you are the only person you can blame. Once you adopt this mentality, you start to have a sense of accountability. You are responsible for your success, but it does not come without preparation.

Sacrifice

Sacrifice and discipline are two things that cannot be compromised if you want to make your dreams a reality. Are you fully invested in your goal or just half way there? Are you one foot in and the other foot elsewhere? You need to be all in if you want to be one of the successful few that go on to earn a scholarship. Once you understand how hard it is to achieve and what it takes to get there, all that is left to do is make a decision. Who are you going to become? How much are you willing to commit?

"The road to success is always under construction." Lily Tomlin

As you start to make progress, the journey never becomes easier. Each milestone you reach, it becomes even more difficult to reach the next. Some of you may need to reinvent yourself to become the person you need to be. If you're not a morning person and feel that you're unable to change that, then I have some news for you. You are also unable to make it through college. Early mornings and late nights are going to be the minimum required to have any chance of not only making it to college, but also having success.

Sacrifice comes in many forms. Are you able to sacrifice your ego for the greater cause? When coaches ridicule you and overlook you, are you able to separate your feelings from your ability to work hard? You're going to have to sacrifice a lot, and you will have to make a lot of changes to who you are in order to achieve something you've never done.

Resilience

Resilience is defined as the capacity to recover quickly from difficulties; toughness. The key word here is quickly. The quicker you are able to bounce back, the more resilient you are. We have a term we use in basketball called "short term memory." This can be used in reference to a shooting performance, how well you played in a game or even how poorly you played. It's the ability to move on, regardless of the circumstance. When you have a bad performance in a game, dwelling on this will not benefit you in any way. Yes, giving yourself an analysis is helpful, but feeling down for a long period of time will only delay the process of getting back on your feet and correcting your wrongs the next time you play. Even taking a bad shot or getting a turnover in a game. These are parts of the game. Your coach won't want you to cry about it. Keep playing and forget about it. Short term memory.

Coaches know that players are not perfect. As high as their expectations are, they don't expect anyone to play a perfect game all the time. We are all human. If you lose focus after making mistakes and it disrupts your play after, then it says a lot about your resilience. It's not just for when you make mistakes, though. Even if you have a good performance, you should not dwell on this for too long. You should never be too high after a victory or too low after a defeat. Remember that there is always work to be done. Resilience is so crucial if you are to make it as far as you wish to. Many things will not only get tested, but also questioned on the road to getting a scholarship. Your resilience is what will determine if you will be able to adapt to any situation and stay the course.

Consistency

"Consistent action creates consistent results." This quote by Christine Kane should be the compass of your life. Everything you read in this book will be completely pointless if you don't intend to apply it on a consistent basis. It's one thing to put the work in, but it's a completely different thing to put in the work night in and night out. Sadly, some of you see working hard as a burden. Keep thinking this way and you won't see the results. If you are serious about working towards a dream, you cannot view hard work in this way. You need to reach a point where you are obsessed with the whole process. Not just the feeling and taste of success, but the grind of putting your body on the line, investing your whole energy into achieving the one goal. Being so obsessed that nobody can take your dream from you. Being obsessed will change the way you think, the way you train and the way you perform. Once you are able to reach this state, complacency has no room.

There you have it, my 5 most important tips. All that is left now is for you to go out and take care of business. Remember that the dream is free, but the hustle is sold separately. Always dream big, but always make sure that your hard work matches your ambitions. The only thing getting in the way of your goals is you yourself. My biggest hope is someone reading this book wants to prove themselves so much they are willing to do what it takes to achieve anything they set their mind to doing. As you continue to excel and destroy each goal one at a time, your hard work and dedication will be infectious to the people around you. You, then, become an example and role model to your teammates, friends and even your coaches. Next time you're alone by yourself on the court and you're counting down the last few seconds, look your imaginary defender in the eyes. Release the shot to the sound of the net swishing and the crowd screaming. Hold onto that feeling and remember that it is possible. It's possible because you believed it was.

Bibliography

Sources

https://www.sportspromedia.com/news/ncaa-basketball-rule-changes-agents-corruption

http://fs.ncaa.org/Docs/eligibility_center/Student_Resources/Registration_Checklist.pdf

http://www.ncaa.org/student-athletes/future/how-register

https://www.athleticscholarships.net/academic-requirements.htm

https://www.statista.com/statistics/267942/participation-in-us-high-school-basketball/

http://www.ncaa.org/about/resources/research/estimated-probability-competing-college-athletics

https://www.heacademy.ac.uk/system/files/resources/Guide%20on%20grade%20point%20average%20for%20students_0.pdf

http://www.ncaa.org/student-athletes/current/transfer-terms

https://www.naia.org/student-athletes/benefits/transfer

http://www.ucsports-canada.com/basketball.html

Printed in Great Britain
by Amazon